The Ants Go Marching

■SCHOLASTIC

Children's Press®
A Division of Scholastic Inc.
New York Toronto London Auckland Sydney Mexico City
New Delhi Hong Kong Danbury, Connecticut

Early Childhood Consultants:

Ellen Booth Church
Diane Ohanesian

1 2 3 4 5 6 7 8 9 10 R 19 18 17 16 15 14 13 12 11 10   62
Library of Congress Cataloging-in-Publication Data

The ants go marching.
   p. cm. — (Rookie preschool)
   Summary: New lyrics to the classic song introduce such common insects as the grasshopper, ladybug, and bee.
   ISBN-13: 978-0-531-24406-7 (lib. bdg.)   ISBN-13: 978-0-531-24581-1 (pbk.)
   ISBN-10: 0-531-24406-7   (lib. bdg.)   ISBN-10: 0-531-24581-0 (pbk.)

1. Children's songs, English—United States—Texts. [1. Insects—Songs and music.
2. Songs.] I. Title. II. Series.

PZA.3.A552 2010
782.42 – dc22   2009005791

Ants go marching.
Let's count one.

Hurrah!

Hurrah!

Ants go marching.
Let's count one.

Hurrah!

Hurrah!

1

3

Ants go marching one by one,
underneath the hot, hot sun.

And they all go marching, marching on their way.

Grasshoppers go jumping.
Let's count two.

Hurrah!

Hurrah!

2

Grasshoppers go jumping.
Let's count two.

Hurrah! Hurrah!

Grasshoppers go jumping
two by two,
underneath the sky so blue.

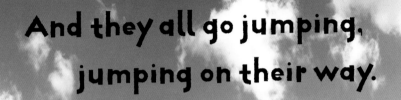

And they all go jumping,
jumping on their way.

Ladybugs go crawling.
Let's count three.

Hurrah!

Hurrah!

Ladybugs go crawling.
Let's count three.

Hurrah!

Hurrah!

Ladybugs go crawling
three by three,
underneath a
great big tree.

12

And they all go crawling,
crawling on their way.

Caterpillars go creeping.
Let's count four.

Hurrah!
Hurrah!

4

Caterpillars go creeping.
Let's count four.

Hurrah!

Hurrah!

Caterpillars go creeping
four by four,
 all along the forest floor.

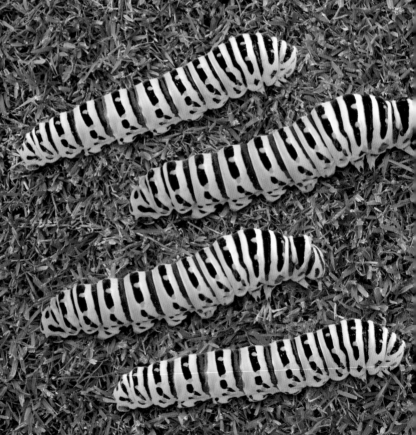

And they all go creeping,
creeping on their way.

Bees go flying.
Let's count five.

Hurrah!

Hurrah!

Bees go flying.

Let's count five.

Hurrah!

Hurrah!

5

Bees go flying five by five,
flying to their honey hive.

And they
all go flying,
flying on
their way.

Hurrah!

1 Ant goes marching

2 Grasshoppers go jumping

3 Ladybugs go crawlin

5
Bees go flying

4
Caterpillars go creeping

Rookie Storytime Tips

. . . .

The Ants Go Marching offers a delightful new version of a familiar preschool song. As you read this book with your child, be sure to stop and count the insects on the pages that introduce the numerals 1–5. As you count together, you'll reinforce one-to-one correspondence, a key early math skill.

. . . .

Invite your preschooler to go back through the book and find and count the following. You will be reinforcing counting skills as well as recognition of backyard insects, which are both part of the preschool curriculum.

Where are the grasshoppers jumping?

 Where are the ladybugs crawling?

 What are the bees flying toward?

Ask your child if he or she can march like an ant? Jump like a grasshopper? Crawl like a ladybug? Creep like a caterpillar? Fly like a bee?